SIMPLE
MEDITATION

Meditation is a practice,

a process, and a state of being.

It is a vehicle for bringing us

'home' to our true Self

Anna Voigt

For Sinclair, and the memory
of my mother, 'Glad'

SIMPLE
MEDITATION

for everyday relaxation
and rejuvenation

ANNA VOIGT

BARNES
&NOBLE
BOOKS
NEW YORK

CONTENTS

INTRODUCTION

'In the beginner's mind there are many possibilities,
but in the expert's there are few'
Shunryu Suzuki

The essential purpose of meditation is to attain inner balance and harmony through the integration of body, mind and soul, leading to greater Self-Realization. The techniques of meditation are profoundly simple but have far-reaching benefits to overall health and well-being — from tension relaxation and stress reduction to increased self-awareness, clarity and peace of mind.

For many people, the meditative state has long been associated with statues of serene-looking Buddhas, seen in museums and picture reproductions, sitting in cross-legged postures with downcast eyes and dignified dispositions. These statues seemed far removed from our own lives and experiences. However, in more recent times we have learned that meditation has not only been a practice of Buddhism for around 2,500 years, but reaches back to our earliest ancestors — the shamans of hunter-gatherer civilizations — and has been practiced in Hinduism (which gave birth to Buddhism) for around 5,000 years. Meditation has also existed for some time in the mystical practices of all of the world's major religions, East and West. It is practiced in the Kabbalah of Judaism, Christian mysticism, and the Sufism of Islam.

Today, the practice of meditation is no longer confined to the temples, synagogues, churches and mosques, and is regularly practiced all over the world. People practice wherever and whenever they can — at home, in the garden, in the wild, in the park, and in the office. They practice individually at home and/or in groups. Meditation has entered the stream of everyday life — where it essentially belongs. As meditation has become more widely practiced, its beneficial power has become increasingly well known and documented.

The power of meditation is the potential held within its profoundly simple but effective techniques. This is the potential to transform lives, irrespective of physical, cultural or economic circumstances. Meditation knows no boundaries.

Although many different meditation practices exist, all that is needed for the basic practice of meditation is contained within our bodies: our ability to quietly turn our attention inwards and to consciously focus and concentrate on our breathing for a small amount of time each day.

This free gift of peace, quiet and solitude, which is always available to us, can transform our lives from dis-ease to ease, from depression to creative expression, from anxiety to serenity, from lethargy to vitality, from contention to inner liberation.

SIMPLE MEDITATION BASICS
The benefits of meditation for the mind, body and soul

As long as you can breathe, you can meditate — it is really that simple.

Meditation can be seen as an opportunity to take a short vacation from the external world to renew our systems and to stay in touch with our real needs and feelings. Even brief respites from daily demands can replenish a tired body, settle our emotions and nervous systems, and give our cluttered, overloaded minds a much-needed rest. And making a priority of time simply to be with ourselves is a form of self-respect, a way of valuing our needs, which has a positive effect on self-esteem.

Like our ancestors, we share the age-old human aspirations for personal, family and social security, good health, sufficient understanding and competent work skills that offer the hope of a fulfilling life. And we also share the challenges and difficulties that invariably arise in trying to satisfy these needs and desires. However, the unprecedented speed of change in contemporary cultures has compounded the ordinary, but difficult enough, human challenges and dilemmas.

The constant adjustments required to survive in today's world have greatly increased the amount of stress people experience in their daily lives. And while change continues unchecked, techniques to assist people's bodies, minds and psyches to cope with the fallout of rampant 'development' have not kept pace with human need. The result is increasing numbers of stress-related, psycho-physical illnesses and environmentally-related health problems.

There is also growing evidence in our societies of chronic anxiety-related disorders, extreme and inappropriate aggression, depression, and various forms of drug dependency and other depleting addictions. The temporary gratification offered by material wealth does not disguise, and is perhaps even the cause of, underlying feelings of malaise and spiritual impoverishment.

While there are no instant cures or easy solutions to redress these imbalances, particularly on a large scale, some simple techniques exist that can be individually learned to improve one's health and general sense of well-being. This alone gives us a greater personal sense of empowerment.

Meditation, whose basis is using the breath to maximum effect, is not only the easiest to learn of the available natural health methods, it is also one of the most efficient and effective. It has been tried, refined and proven true over many, many centuries.

Simple meditation techniques are accessible to everyone; you can begin right here, right now, and notice benefits within a relatively short period. And maybe one day, you might even find that the satisfaction you were seeking outside yourself has been inside you all the time. All it costs is an open mind, a little of your time, and your willingness to make a regular commitment.

Like the rediscovery of a precious relic hidden beneath layers of dirt, you rediscovered your true self, your real identity, which had been buried and forgotten in the depths of your unconscious.
Pir Vilayat Inayat Khan

Meditation simplifies life in providing a space to shift from thinking to sensing ... it enables us to hear our intuition and to discover the beauty that resides in 'stillness' and 'silence.'

Different meditation styles

Many different styles of meditation are available, so you can experiment and discover which ones 'fit.' It is best to maintain one particular technique as your basic practice, and to augment it with other forms when you feel a particular need, or seek to expand your experience through another perspective.

As well as a basic or beginning meditation practice, usually focused on the breath (*see* 'Setting up to Meditate' and 'Breathing and Meditation' on pages 16–33), various 'still' and active meditations can also be utilized. Some of these will be discussed in later chapters; however, a sense of each style may be helpful for you to decide how you will set up a meditation space.

Some people prefer to meditate on a specific object. This could be a picture of a beautiful natural scene, a respected teacher, an image of something one aspires to, or even an image of a loved animal.

Another object that holds great attraction for meditators is the simple beauty of a candle flame. Not only does candle light exude a wonderful aura, the symbolism it contains holds much potency: its flickering can represent thoughts and a ready availability to distraction, while its steady burning can represent a calm, centered stillness.

A widely used ancient technique is to utilize the power of sound as a doorway into the meditative state. The most commonly used sound form is the repetition of a *mantra*, which is a specific, meaningful word or phrase.

Music is inherently meditation material, and you can use any composition with which you have an affinity (*see* 'A selection of music for meditation, relaxation and healing' on page 51).

Fragrant, natural substances and their vapor have been an accompaniment to religious rites and festivals from prehistoric times continously into the present. Today, essential oils used in aromatherapy are burned in meditative practices. Aroma and sound can be used together.

Colors associated with the *chakras* — subtle energy centers in the body — can be used as a focus for meditation. The hues of a rainbow can become tools for practice, and

'color breathing' can be an effective cleansing and healing agent. Meditation on a mandala and its symbolism is a traditional practice which also has some contemporary variations.

For those who find it difficult or counterproductive to sit still, walking meditations and other movement practices might be preferable. A practice of meditative walking through a labyrinth has become a novel Western variant on the walking meditation and the labyrinthine puzzle. Focused dancing can also be a wonderful meditation.

There is a meditation practice available to suit all dispositions. It then becomes a personal decision whether to practice or not. Meditation is simple, but it is not easy, and needs commitment for its benefits to manifest themselves — as with most forms of achievement.

It may be important to mention that meditation is not intended to be approached in a heavy or serious way. Over time, you will witness many moments of humor and joy as well as uncover disquieting concerns. A cheerful attitude, a sense of humor and an openness to discovery are of invaluable assistance on this adventurous voyage. It is also best undertaken as a life-long commitment, so you need to travel lightly! Keep your meditation simple, to minimize possible periodic temptations to abandon practice, particularly when the weight of emotional baggage invariably arises.

And remember, meditation is, after all, a respite from the external world as well as potentially one of the greatest gifts you can ever give to yourself. However, no matter how much you read about meditation, its benefits cannot begin until you begin to practice it yourself.

Letting go of the distractions of everyday life

The meditative practice of simply attending to oneself while letting go of the wearisome miscellanea of thoughts that constantly bombard and preoccupy us — even for a few precious minutes a day — helps us to gain a healthier perspective and release much unnecessary daily trivia.

By not allowing our energies to be scattered, by letting our thoughts, minor discomforts, and demanding emotions go — in each and every moment — we learn to let other unimportant things go. We also come to realize that the coming and going of phenomena is the very nature of worldly existence. This realization can help us accept and cope with the inevitable losses in our lives.

Over time, meditation practices assist in establishing a sense of internal strength, confidence and well-being in practitioners. With practice, meditation integrates body, mind and soul, bestowing that expanded sense of health and well-being that we experience when all the parts of ourselves are working as harmonious units, each supporting each, as in a chamber orchestra.

Relaxation

To be able to relax is an essential component of effective meditation. To relax and meditate, even for only ten minutes a day, can produce tangible benefits. Physical discomforts can be gently eased, which results in a tension-free body wherein energy can flow more freely. This increases vitality and flexibility. A relaxed body calms the mind — and vice versa — which eases the spirit.

Breathing relaxation methods used in meditation produce an overall calming effect, which can reduce anxiety and help in managing pain. Deep respiration techniques can correct faulty breathing habits, while increasing the intake of oxygen into the lungs — which are seldom used to their maximum potential. Considerable research attests to benefits for asthma sufferers. Overall, more efficient use of oxygen in our systems can increase energy and enhance physical and mental endurance.

The combination of meditation and yoga (*see* pages 34–43) has proven particularly successful in decreasing pain levels in chronic sufferers. Relaxation also has a regulatory effect on our nervous systems, metabolism and digestion. It improves our cardiac function and circulation. Concrete physical results can be seen in reducing high blood pressure (hypertension), combating heart disease, treating peptic ulcers, reducing tension headaches and promoting more restful sleep. The ability to consciously relax also appears to have a beneficial effect on our immune systems.

The emphasis on relaxation and breathing techniques in yoga and meditation, as well as the conscious attention to inner experience and development, are not usually incorporated into other relaxation and exercise techniques.

Mindfulness

*In 'insight (Vipassana) meditation,' the path begins with
mindfulness (satipatthana), proceeds through insight (vipassana)
and ends in enlightenment (nirvana).*

 Regular practice of *any* meditation technique can be effective in modifying the way we respond to stress. Indeed, the longer meditation is practiced, the more relaxed people become. However, what is unique about meditation, compared to other forms of relaxation, is that meditators also become more *alert*.

Meditation nurtures this powerful state of relaxation with alertness because it trains practitioners to be attentive and to notice whatever arises *in the moment*. This deliberate attention, presence and acceptance of what one is experiencing from moment to moment is termed *'mindfulness'* in Buddhism. It is a core principle of meditation practice, a skill that, once developed, spills over into everyday life and can be applied to just about every activity and every situation.

For a Zen Buddhist practitioner, for example, to be mindful is simply to be exactly and fully where she or he is now — recognizing that, whatever else the mind may say, the present moment is the only time we really have. Whether sitting in stillness meditation or walking in the street, the attention of Zen practitioners is firmly focused on what they are doing — if eating, they eat, if working, they work, and so on. The present moment, being life itself, is seen as far too precious to miss.

The practice of mindfulness also has a way of simplifying life, and helps us not to continue to grasp and cling to everyday reactions and material objects. The way it does this is by teaching us to focus on one major object of attention, releasing everything else. This in itself, as well as developing focus and concentration, is helpful in learning to discriminate between what is important and what is just habitual and peripheral in our lives.

To be mindful does not mean not to think, or plan, or remember. It just means that we need to be consciously aware of what we are thinking, what we are planning, and what we are remembering at the time of engaging with these processes. Also, we need to direct these processes, rather than having them be a distraction or avoidance of the present moment or of the true reality of our lives.

Although ultimately rewarding, facing the reality of your own life without excuses or props takes a little courage and persistence. A way to enjoy the process is to make the discovery of your Self a real adventure, and/or to forget it is about your self at all — imagine that you are simply learning about a very fascinating human being.

*Day and night, be aware
with each breath,
and live there*
Lalla

*Meditate within eternity
Don't stay in the mind
Your thoughts are like a child fretting near its mother's breast, restless
and afraid, who with a little guidance, can find the path of courage*
Lalla

SETTING UP TO MEDITATE

Meditation is not concentration. It is simple awareness! You simply relax and watch the breathing. In that watching, nothing is excluded. The car is humming — perfectly okay, accept it. The traffic is passing — that's okay, part of life. The fellow passenger snoring by your side — accept it. Nothing is rejected.

O s h o

In setting up your meditation, a few basic considerations are helpful to support your practice.

Appoint a regular time and place

The early morning is generally perceived to be the most beneficial time to practice. At this time, the body is (one hopes) rested and relaxed from sleep, the stomach is empty, and a new day is beginning, so approaching activities and demands have not yet impinged much on the mind. Meditation also helps to center us, which gives an inner strength and clarity that can carry us through the day ahead. If early morning is not a feasible proposition, other good times to meditate are at noon, twilight, midnight, or before going to bed. The important principle here is to decide upon a regular time that is manageable and stick to it.

Minimum time

Once a time has been set, initially allow at least ten minutes for your meditation practice. This is really the minimum time needed for the body and mind to settle, to establish your meditation routine, and for benefits to be felt. Do keep to this time, no matter how restless, distracted or bored you become. As your meditation deepens, you may wish to extend the time, but allow this to happen naturally.

Relaxation is essential for effective meditation

A few stretches, coupled with some deep breath releases, helps relax the body before commencing meditation. Relaxation exercises in themselves are very effective in releasing tension, as well as in managing stress. They can also loosen up stiff joints if this is a problem (*see* 'Simple relaxation exercise one' on page 20).

Posture

In determining your posture, the most important factor is that your body is stable and comfortable enough to maintain the posture, with a minimum of movement, for the duration of the meditation. To be distracted by discomfort is counterproductive. It is essential to keep your spine as erect as possible, in one line with your neck and head — with your chin tucked in slightly.

You can sit cross-legged on the floor, on a reasonably firm cushion, or in a chair — without leaning against its back. A round, firm cushion specifically created for meditation, called a *zafu*, is sold at many stores, and you can also purchase meditation stools from specialty outlets.

If sitting on a chair, you need to place both feet on the floor and not cross your legs. You can imagine yourself as a connection between heaven and earth. Your seat represents your groundedness on the earth, and the crown of your head is symbolically holding up the sky. Your body is the pillar of support maintaining the connection.

Focus of attention

Either close your eyes or turn your gaze downwards. Whether your eyes are closed or slightly open, your focus remains soft and directed inwards — unless you are meditating on an exterior object. Whatever the object of your attention, be it the breath, an image or sound, you peripherally notice, accept, and let go of passing thoughts, feelings and sensations.

Clothing

Clothing should be loose-fitting and comfortable. Natural-fiber fabrics are preferable, as they allow the body to breathe. Ensure that you are warm enough if the temperature is cool. If you wish, you can use a special shawl or some other garment which signifies to you that you are entering into meditation.

Meditation space

Very few of us have the luxury of a meditation room or a study that can also serve as meditation space. Other options include a specific place — such as a corner of a room, perhaps in your bedroom — that you can set up however you wish, where you can sit comfortably and meditate regularly without being disturbed. If you choose to meditate in your bedroom, it is preferable not to do so while lying in bed, because of the association with sleep and the strong possiblity of nodding off. If your bed is the only option, sit rather than lie down. Whatever space you choose, it needs to be kept clean and tidy and, if possible, reserved for meditation use.

Setting up an altar

Many people like to set up a small altar of meaningful objects, such as pictures, incense sticks or an essential oil burner, candles, a plant, or a vase of fresh flowers. Perhaps choose one item from each category to avoid clutter, so that objects do not vie for your attention in the same way as your thoughts! The benefit of your reserved 'sacred space' is that over time, your body and psyche become acclimatized to the space and more quickly move into the meditative alpha state. The space also becomes charged with the energy generated by meditation.

On meditation techniques

Once you have chosen a meditation technique, it is best to stick with it for several weeks or preferably months before further experimenting with other methods. In this way you can determine in which ways specific techniques benefit you.

Open attitude

To get the maximum benefit from your meditation, each time you meditate, approach the practice with an open mind and heart. If you wish, connect with whatever it is that brings you to meditate, then drop any preconceptions and expectations whatsoever of what should or should not happen. Apart from the basics to support you, there is no right or wrong in this process.

Letting go

While meditating, pay attention to what arises in each succesive moment and accept all as simply 'what is,' always coming back to, and holding, the object of concentration — i.e., the practice of *mindfulness*. Do not hold on to perceived 'bad' or 'good' moments, but allow all moments to pass. Let go of your ego-self. My late father-in-law was fond of the Christian epithet 'Man proposes, God disposes.' My late mother often said 'God works in mysterious ways.' You get the notion. We are all imperfect beings in an imperfect world — and let that go too!

Dealing with thoughts

Do not suppress your thoughts, but when they arise, notice them and then dispel them. You can let them simply dissolve, release them in 'bubbles,' tell them you are occupied right now, or name them and release them. Be sure to come back to your focus of concentration continually.

On self-acceptance and compassion

Meditation is not intended as a system of self- or other-judgement, but as a process that calms the mind, reduces stress, increases self-awareness and offers freedom from the bondage of ingrained habits of self-limiting thought and behavior. The purpose of meditation is to help us find our true selves. So be kind, gentle, patient and warmly compassionate towards yourself — as you are with a loved friend. And try to keep your sense of humor alive.

Remember the setting and meditation techniques are not ends in themselves; they are only technical support for establishing a meditation *practice*.

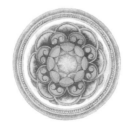

Three simple relaxation exercises

Simple Relaxation Exercise One:

◆ Give your body a good wiggle and shake all over.

◆ Then reach for the sky with your hands while inhaling and standing on your toes.

◆ Then let your arms loosely fall to the ground in front of your body while you rapidly exhale.

◆ Imagine releasing all the negativity in your body on the exhalation.

◆ Let your arms hang loosely in this position for a moment or so.

◆ Repeat two more times.

Simple Relaxation Exercise Two:

Abdominal breathing: a simple yoga exercise:

◆ Lie flat on your back in what is called the *corpse pose* (shavasana), with legs straight and feet slightly apart. Place arms and hands a little distance from your body with palms facing upward (for a full description of this posture and its benefits, *see* 'Yoga and Meditation' on pages 34–43).

◆ Take a few deep breaths directly into your abdomen, exaggerating its upward movement.

◆ Slowly release the breath from the abdomen to your collarbone.

◆ Repeat a few times.

◆ When finished, turn onto your right side for a moment or two.

◆ Move to your meditation place and seat (if possible).

Practice note: This breathing motion is a reversal of our usual pattern of breathing first into our chests. It is a very efficient way to relax quickly at any time, and is particularly useful in stressful circumstances. It is also a first step to correcting poor breathing habits — particularly the (usually unconscious) shallow breathing of most people.

Simple Relaxation Exercise Three:

This is an exercise that involves tensing, then releasing muscles.

Below are two versions of this commonly practiced technique:

◆ Lie flat on your back in the corpse posture (see Relaxation Exercise Two).

◆ Inhale naturally and deeply from your abdomen to your chest.

◆ Tense all the muscles that you can in your body.

◆ Hold for a few seconds.

◆ Exhale and release the tension from your muscles.

General practice note: This exercise can be extended to tensing and relaxing individual parts of your body, beginning with the scalp muscles and working down through all the musculature to the toes, left side of the body first, then up the right side. This is a great exercise done prior to sleeping and/or after a stressful day. Whatever preliminary exercise you use, always relax the body on the exhalation. So: inhale, tense, exhale and release. Meditation always focuses greater attention on the outgoing breath, to dissolve and release.

Ten-minute easy meditation

Simple breathing meditation

1. Select a quiet space — a corner of a room, somewhere in a garden or park — where you will not be interrupted for the duration of your meditation.

2. Allow yourself ten minutes for your meditation, preceded by a few minutes of relaxation time (*see* 'Three simple relaxation exercises' on pages 20–21). If it helps you relax, have soft music playing in the background.

3. Sit in a comfortable position on a floor cushion or chair. Loosen any parts of your clothing that inhibit the natural flow of your breath, or prevent you from sitting comfortably. Ensure your spine is gently erect, and your back, neck and head are aligned. Tuck your chin in a little, and soften your facial muscles. Rest your hands, palms down, gently on your thighs, or place your right hand in your left, palms up, and hold below your belly. Relax your mouth and leave it slightly open. Close your eyes, take a couple of deep breaths and exhale fully through the nose. Continue to inhale and exhale through the nose for the duration of your meditation.

4. Take a moment to note your motivation for meditating. This can help to focus your concentration. With repeated practice, this can also serve to reaffirm your purpose and commitment when difficulties arise.

5. Turn your attention from your thoughts and the surrounding sounds to your body. Notice your posture and, if there is discomfort, make any necessary adjustments, then try not to move. Scan your body; if there is any tension, breathe into it and release it on the out-breath. Note the stillness of your body and allow yourself to sink into that stillness.

6. Now consciously focus on the breath. Choose a place in your body where the breathing is particularly noticeable — at the tip of the nostrils where breath enters the body, in the middle of the chest or in the belly. Experiment with a couple of breaths in each area to see which feels most comfortable and where you breathe most easily. This is your point of concentration for the duration of your meditation.

7. Inhale and exhale into the part of your body you have chosen to focus on. Breathe as naturally as possible — do not force anything. Notice the breath entering and leaving that part of the body, as well as the space in between. Notice the body expanding and contracting with the breath. Notice the oneness of your body and breath.

8. As thoughts, sensations, and emotions arise, note them, and either let them dissolve or give them a tag and then release them, all the time focusing on the breath in your body. If you get lost in a train of thought, or immersed in an emotion, or captured by a sensation, notice it and immediately return to your breathing — without reprimand. The mind has long had a free run, so most likely will not be reined in without a tussle.

9. When your meditation time has come to a close, gently bring yourself back to your surroundings by noticing your body, then the energy around you, and then the surrounding sounds. Give thanks for this peaceful time and space. Move forward in your day.

BREATHING AND MEDITATION

Becoming conscious of your breathing

When the mind is kept on the breath, even for a few minutes,
the body will relax.

Breath is life, life is breath. Breath influences even the microscopic processes of our bodies, such as the activities of our cells. It is also closely linked with the performance of our brains. Respiration is the fuel that burns oxygen and glucose, producing the energy to mobilize every glandular secretion, every muscular contraction, every activity of our brain function. Traditional peoples revered the breath as the life force itself. Nothing in life is more powerful than the breath, yet most of us are unaware of our breathing, simply taking it for granted.

Many people assume that because breathing is a semi-automatic function, it is beyond our active control. This is not so. Although breathing is largely an unconscious process, we can take conscious control of the breath at any time. Consequently, the breath becomes a bridge between the conscious and unconscious dimensions of our minds.

Becoming conscious of our breath, and our existing breathing patterns, and to be able to use our breath to release blockages and stress, gives us the key to relaxing our body and mind. This also gives us some control over the quality of our lives. And the beauty of the breath is that it is always available to us.

Basic meditation practices usually focus on the breath, aiming to calm the mind and reduce distractions, as practices in themselves or before engaging in other forms of meditation. Deep-breathing relaxation techniques also can be done separately, whenever needed, or used just prior to meditation.

Through meditation, the magic that is breathing comes into conscious awareness. We become acquainted with our normal breathing patterns and experience how they affect our bodies and minds. Meditation practice teaches that the breath follows the movement of mind and vice versa. Through purposeful use of your breath you can learn to control your mind. To be able to travel inwards consciously on your breath to discover self-knowledge is simply one of the most powerful things you can do to increase self-awareness.

Life is literally dependent on breath. As well as sustaining our lives, more than any other single phenomenon, the breath holds a key to transformation.

The breath mirrors our state of being in any given moment. Stop *right now*, and check your breathing — without changing anything. Immediately after this, check in with yourself and note what you are doing, what you are thinking, what are the sensations in your body and what you are feeling. Don't think about it, don't censor anything, don't change anything. If you do find yourself instantly moved to change something, notice what that 'something' is. Accept whatever comes to your attention. This is a simple but very effective exercise in awareness that can be done anywhere, anytime.

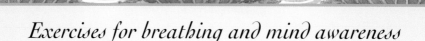

Exercises for breathing and mind awareness

Breath counting

◆ Begin by sitting in a position that you can comfortably hold for ten minutes.

◆ Ensure that your spine, neck and head are in alignment, yet relaxed.

◆ Rest your hands gently on your thighs, with elbows beside your body.

◆ Take a few deep breaths and slowly exhale.

◆ Breathe through your nose if you can, with your lips slightly apart.

◆ Breathe as naturally as possible — try not to control your breath in any way, allowing it to find its own rhythm and depth.

◆ Begin counting each in-breath and each out-breath either by:

Counting one to ten — mentally saying 'one' on the inhalation and 'two' on the exhalation, 'three' on the next inhalation, 'four' on the next exhalation, continuing until you reach ten, and then return to 'one' — counting continuously until the ten minutes is up. If you lose your place (which most people do in the beginning stages), do not be concerned, simply return to number one and recommence the cycle.

OR

Counting one to four — saying 'one' on the inhalation and 'one' on the exhalation, 'two' on the inhalation and 'two' on the exhalation, and so on. Continue until you reach four, then return to one. As above, continue the cycle until the time is up. If your attention strays, simply return each time to one and continue.

OR

Breathe on even counts of four — i.e., breathe in to the count of four, hold the breath to the count of four, exhale to the count of four, hold to the count of four, inhale to the count of four, and so on.

Try each method, choosing the one that feels most comfortable. These are good exercises for keeping the attention on the breath. The exercises help to develop concentration, and provide an in-built format that reminds you when your attention is straying. They are also helpful preliminary practices to other breathing meditations, such as following and/or exploring your breath. Try one of these exercises for a few weeks and notice what happens with your mind and body.

Meditation and respiratory problems

Combined with controlled breathing techniques, meditation has proved particularly effective in countering poor and shallow breathing, and in countering respiratory problems such as hayfever and asthma (*see* 'General guidelines for pranayama practices' on pages 42–43).

Asthmatics often experience even regular breathing to be constricted or wheezy, and such discomfort can give rise to negative feelings about breathing itself, as well as to dislike of the illness. A frequent consequence is that to avoid these uncomfortable sensations, an asthmatic attempts to breathe as minimally as possible, which only intensifies the constriction.

When people with respiratory problems learn controlled breathing techniques and meditation, they often experience how much better their breathing can feel. Once they are familiar with the feeling of relaxed breathing, they are better able to evoke it at will, and thus use it when necessary. Even learning simply to relax and breathe more deeply and naturally can have a positive cumulative effect over time.

Stress, anxiety and fear

To be alive is to sometimes feel anxiety and fear. In addition to the 'existential angst' of being human (who are we? why are we here? what is the meaning and purpose of life?), anxiety is a common human response to change, uncertainty, and the unknown. The majority of people also experience fear in reaction to a perceived threat.

A certain amount of stress is necessary to healthy human functioning, and anxiety is a natural reaction to life's ups and downs. Though worry and anxiety are not confined to perceptions of possible negative change, even apparently positive change can make us feel anxious. And our own expectations, and those of others, are invariably present in most interactions.

However, with a complex and constantly changing world, more and more people are displaying symptoms of underlying fear and anxiety, and stress-related health disorders appear to be escalating at an alarming rate.

This can signify disordered perception and that life is out of balance. It also suggests that many people perceive a loss of control over important aspects of their lives. While we can work to change exterior conditions, there is no guarantee that we will make an impact. Moreover, we cannot change other people, no matter how much energy we expend on the attempt.

However, we can change how we perceive situations, and we can work on changing our inner functioning, which in turn influences our behavior. And the simplest place to begin is with our breathing.

When we are worried, fearful or anxious:

Our breathing becomes constricted, shallow, and rapid.

Our heart rate increases.

Our blood pressure rises.

Our body heats up.

Stomach acid increases.

The blood supply returns to the vital organs.

Our muscles become tense and/or tremble.

These are symptoms of the 'fight or flight' response of the body to stress — the central nervous system on 'red alert.'

By contrast, when stress is released and we are relaxed:

Our breathing is slower, more expansive and deeper — more in our abdomen.

Our heart rate returns to normal.

Our blood pressure falls, our blood sugar decreases.

Stomach acidity is regulated, blood flow to gut tissue returns to normal.

The circulation increases to the periphery.

Our muscles loosen.

If our anxieties and fears do not find adequate and healthy release, this results in the body sustaining a chronic level of stress response, and physical and mental discomfort can lead to ailments such as respiratory disorders; gut disorders; peptic ulcers; chronic muscle tension and/or spasm; hypertension (high blood pressure), which is a common cause of strokes and cardiac-related disorders; severe headaches, migraine; depression; insomnia; nervous disorders, neuroses; chronic anxiety and panic attacks.

Three things have proved to be very effective counteragents to the symptoms of anxiety, fear, and stress: controlled deep-breathing exercises, other relaxation techniques, and meditation.

Using the breath to manage fear and anxiety

An increasing number of people are reporting symptoms of chronic anxiety such as panic attacks. These attacks can be frightening to experience, as they often seem to come out of nowhere. Generally though, they are symptomatic of underlying problems.

Most people's breathing is ordinarily very shallow. In addition, when a person is feeling anxious, the breathing becomes even more constricted. In a panic attack, one of the pronounced symptoms is that the breath becomes temporarily frozen on the in-breath and/or the person hyperventilates (fast, short intakes of breath), which can have alarming effects. These are simple illustrations of how the breath is an important and reliable barometer of a person's state of being.

Although a panic attack may be short-lived, it is such a debilitating experience that it can wound a person's self-esteem, and create additional fear and anxiety about its likely reoccurrence, as well as potential embarrassment. A number of techniques for managing anxiety and panic exist that are easy to apply. The most immediately useful one is to connect with the laboring breath:

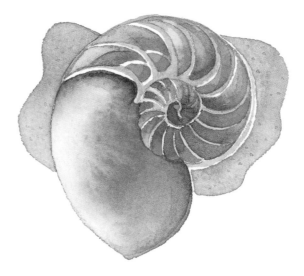

When anxiety, fear, or panic strikes

◆ Gently connect with the breath, and, without the use of force, try to slow the breathing so that it becomes a little more regular.

◆ Pay particular attention to your out-breath, gently relaxing your being with the outflow.

◆ When you feel an ease of tension, a sense of relief and/or release of a sigh, you know you have broken the back of the panic/anxiety.

◆ Maintain the pattern of slow, relaxed, gentle breathing until you once again feel grounded and stable.

Once they recognize that an attack has a tendency to pass quickly, sufferers realize that if they just wait and keep their actions to a minimum, the crisis will pass.

As with other strong emotions, you can use your meditation practice to explore your fears. Over time, you may even transform your fears and anxieties from foes to friends. You may also discover your courage, and the power to connect that lies within ordinary human vulnerability.

Simple meditation for fear and anxiety
(and other strong emotions)

This meditation can also be used in exploring other potent emotions, such as anger, jealousy, resentment, and strong aversions. It can be included in your daily practice or applied in situations in which your fear and anxiety arise.

- Sit in a comfortable position.
- Breathe naturally.
- Begin by asking yourself these questions, and unconditionally accepting any responses and/or resistances:
    - Where do I experience fear and/or anxiety in my body —
      what are the sensations, and where does it tense and contract?
    - What happens to my breathing?
    - What other physical sensations do I experience —
      what happens in my heart area, my throat, and in my head?
    - What typically happens with my voice?

Now turn your attention to your mind:
    - What thoughts usually arise when I feel fear or anxiety?
    - What images present themselves?

With repeated practice, whenever your fear or anxiety returns, you can gently breathe into it, call it by name — fear, fear; anxiety, anxiety, etc., then release it and return to relaxed breathing.

As you further work with the breath in relaxation and meditation, you experience productive ways of using the breath to still your mind and body, which automatically brings a sense of calm. When we feel calm we feel in control. In time, you can learn to respond to stress more effectively, minimizing its harmful effects on your entire system. Before you know it, you will feel happier, more energized, and relaxed enough not to allow life's turbulent surface to ruffle your sense of inner tranquillity!

YOGA AND MEDITATION

History and meaning of yoga

Yoga is severing the connection with that which causes suffering. Yoga should be practiced with insight and with an unperturbed heart.
B h a g a v a d   G i t a   V I : 2 3

Yoga is the complete control of the operations of the mind.
P a t a n j a l i   Y o g a   S u t r a s   1 : 2

Yoga is both an ancient and living Hindu science and philosophy, which extends back through 5,000 years of history in India. It is said to contain the bounty of the teachings of even earlier spiritually advanced civilizations which are lost to contemporary memory. Yoga is one of the very few spiritual traditions which has maintained an unbroken development throughout history. It is also a complete system for integrating body, mind and soul in relationship to the universal forces of Nature, and the boundless Infinite beyond time and space — all of which exist within each human being.

The literal meaning of the Sanskrit word yoga is 'union.' It is derived from the old Sanskrit root *'yuga'* or *'yuj,'* meaning to 'yoke' or 'harness.' It means to 'yoke' together body, mind, and soul, to liberate the true Self. So, yoga can mean either, or both, union and discipline. A system of practices to *relax* the body and mind, yoga's ultimate purpose is to attain Self-Realization or the spontaneous awakening to our original Nature. It is also formulated to assist the practitioner to achieve optimum health and well-being. Thus, yoga can help us fulfil the potential that human life offers us.

The bond of yoga and meditation

Yoga and meditation are inextricably bound. Meditation (*dhyana*) is fundamental to all forms of yoga practice. The Sanskrit word *asana*, which has come to be defined as 'posture,' originally meant 'seat.' Patanjali, an Indian sage who lived in the second century A.D., described it as 'that position which is comfortable and steady' — a posture that would stabilize the body for meditation. The most well-known of the *asanas* is the lotus asana or posture. The ability to keep the body and the mind still for effective meditation is difficult without disciplined and focused practice.

Essential to the development of successful yoga and meditation practice is the ability to let *go* of tension — the tension that arises from our limited ego perception of ourselves as separate entities from other forms of life, and separate from the true Self. Relaxation in this sense is not simply relaxation of the body, but also a calming of the mind, and it is the key to all of the various levels of yogic endeavor.

Knowledge of Eastern religious disciplines of meditation and yoga began filtering into the West about one hundred years ago. Today, meditation and yoga are mainstream, with many pop stars, actresses and actors praising the benefits of these practices.

The simple requirements for meditation and yoga practice make them accessible to anyone who is interested. Despite the prevalent images of yoga practitioners in seemingly difficult postures, yoga, like meditation, can be practiced by anyone, regardless of one's state of health, age or level of physical fitness. You do not need to be fit and flexible before taking up yoga. Many aspects of the ancient yoga techniques can be adapted and applied to individual needs and capacities, but for this you will need an experienced teacher.

Yoga and relaxation

A tension-free body and peaceful, concentrated mind are the result of learning *how* to relax, enabling better management of stressful situations and one's everyday life, as well as work pressures. To be able to enjoy physical relaxation, hatha yoga teaches that it is important to combine both stretching and strengthening *asanas*, because doing stretching exercises only makes muscles become tense and shortened due to strain, as they lack the necessary strength, while doing strengthening exercises only makes muscles lose their flexibility, which becomes increasingly obvious in the decreasing mobility of the joint (i.e., stiff joints).

Combining stretching and strengthening asanas:

♦ Develops important protection for the joints and the spinal column. The importance of a straight and flexible spine has particular emphasis in hatha yoga, and indeed in all yoga schools and practices.

♦ Supplies the necessary stimulus to ligaments, capsules and cartilage for their natural functioning, helping them regain elasticity.

♦ Nourishes the joint with increased production of joint fluid in the inner layer of the joint capsule.

As well as having a favorable effect on muscles and the surrounding structure of the joint (ligaments, capsule, cartilage, discs, menisci), asanas also:

♦ Have a harmonious effect on the organs, glandular system and circulation. The dynamic movements stimulate the circulatory system, which has a regulatory effect on the vital organs and glandular function.

Integral to the effective execution of the *asanas*, and fundamental to yoga practice generally, is correct breathing. In hatha yoga, healthy breathing is nurtured through the controlled breathing techniques of pranayama.

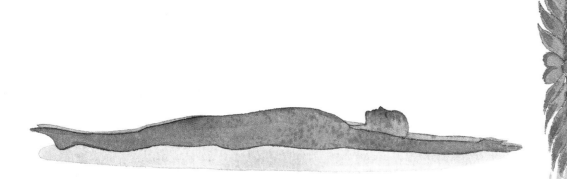

The benefits of yoga

◆ It stretches, strengthens, and tones muscles.
◆ It improves flexibility and range of movement.
◆ It actively eliminates toxins from the body.
◆ It improves respiratory and heart function.
◆ It revitalizes the entire system by removing energy blocks.
◆ It relaxes the whole body.

As with meditation:
◆ It increases the capacity to concentrate.
◆ It develops greater self-awareness of body and mind.
◆ It fosters an enduring sense of well-being, equanimity and inner peace.

One does not have to practice yoga to practice meditation, but yoga does offer some wonderfully beneficial techniques (such as the relaxation and pranayama practices in this book) to assist in the development of relaxation and the attainment of the meditative state.

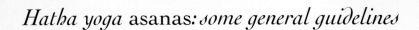

Hatha yoga asanas: *some general guidelines*

- The *asanas* are to be executed precisely and slowly.
- The aim is to relax those muscles involved in performing the individual *asanas*.
- The attention is on the deliberate action of the *asanas* and the breath.
- Always breathe through the nose.
- The breathing technique should be relaxed and natural yogic breathing, i.e. inhaling from the abdomen to the upper chest and exhaling from the upper chest to the abdomen.
- Generally, you inhale during movements in which the chest and abdominal areas are opened and expanded, and exhale during movements that constrict the chest and abdominal areas.
- To relax muscles, concentrate on the tense part of the *asana*, consciously relaxing it with each exhalation.

Hatha yoga asanas *for relaxation and meditation*

1. Corpse pose (shavasana)

This is a wonderfully beneficial posture that relaxes the whole psycho-physiological system. It is used throughout yoga practice — prior to, in between, and especially after the stretching and dynamic *asanas*.

- Lie flat on your back with arms slightly away from your body, with palms facing upward.
- Move your legs slightly apart, let the feet fall to the side, and close your eyes.
- Make sure your spine, neck and head are aligned. Put a flat pillow, or folded cloth, behind your head for comfort, if you wish. Ensure your head does not fall to one side.
- Relax the entire body, and stop all muscular movement.
- Become aware of your natural breathing, and allow the breath to become rhythmic and relaxed.

- ◆ Begin to count your breaths from the number 27 backwards to zero. Mentally say, 'I am breathing in 27, I am breathing out 27, I am breathing in 26, I am breathing out 26' and so on, until you reach zero.
- ◆ As in all breath-counting exercises, if your mind wanders and you forget the next number, bring your attention back to the counting, and start again at 27.

You can do this exercise for a few minutes (in-between *asanas*), or longer if you have time. It can be done as part of your yoga or meditation practice, when you need to relax quickly , or when you are feeling physically and mentally tired. It is an ideal practice just prior to going to sleep.

2. Full body stretch

- ◆ Lie flat on your back, with legs outstretched. Lay your arms on the floor beside the body with elbows straight and palms down. Spine, neck and head are to be in alignment, without tension or strain (*base position*).
- ◆ Inhale naturally from abdomen to chest.
- ◆ Keeping your arms straight, raise them above your head, and stretch as far as you can.
- ◆ At the same time, point your toes, and stretch your legs as far as you can.
- ◆ Feel the stretch in the entire length of your body.
- ◆ Hold for a moment or two, then begin to exhale.
- ◆ Bring your hands back to your sides.
- ◆ Allow your feet to resume their normal position.
- ◆ Relax your body for a moment or two.

Repeat five times, alternating between pointing your toes forward with one inhalation, and, with the next inhalation, pulling your toes back towards your shins. This is a good relaxation exercise to do prior to meditation.

The practice of pranayama

Prananyama or pranayam is a system of hatha yoga breathing practices. The word pranayama comes from *prana* and *ayama*. Prana is the life force, the sustaining life-energy in all phenomena. It is that universal energy current analogous to 'chi' in Tai Chi, or the 'qi' in Qi Gong. 'Yam' means air or breath, and also conscious control.

Although *prana* is sometimes referred to as the breath itself, or as an element, the ancients knew it to be a much more subtle energy that can only be perceived by the very sensitive yoga adept. The majority of us only perceive *prana* as the living form with which it has established a connection, such as the breath, sound, color or material form.

The nature of *prana* is always to flow. When *prana* flows freely throughout the human body, then good health and well-being is enjoyed. However, if the flow of *prana* is obstructed in the body, because of a physical or psycho-physical problem, then poor health and dis-ease are the result. Through a practice of regular breathing patterns, pranayama re-establishes the natural, relaxed rhythms of the body and mind, and can reverse these dis-ease processes.

Prana flows throughout the body via *nadis*, which are like the meridians in Chinese medicine and serve as the basis of practices such as acupuncture. Thousands of *nadis* exist in the human body, operating like subtle channels or nerve pathways, but just like meridians, they are not visible through anatomical dissection. However, modern scientific radiation-tracking techniques are now confirming what the ancients intuitively and sensitively perceived.

In yoga, three principal *nadis* are distinguished from the others. These include the *sushumna nadi* — the central *prana* channel that runs the entire length of the spinal column. The *ida nadi* is the left channel and *pingala nadi* is the right channel, both of which twist around the *sushumna nadi* at the *chakras* (subtle energy centers), in the figure eight pattern reminiscent of DNA.

In pranayama practice, the important aspects of breathing are inhalation, exhalation, and breath retention, with the breathing emphasis on breath retention. However, in the beginning, greater attention is given to inhalation and exhalation to strengthen the lungs and balance the pranic and nervous systems. This prepares the body for the control of respiration necessary in the breath retention practices.

Cautionary note: Generally speaking, pranayama is an advanced set of practices, requiring a stable foundation that can handle the powerful play of subtle energy forces in the system. These practices also need to be performed in the correct manner, so as not to do any damage, and they really need to be learned from an experienced yoga teacher. However, a couple of basic practices can be beneficial for anyone to use, and are helpful for meditation.

Pranayama should not be practiced during illness. However, simple breath awareness and abdominal breathing (*see* 'Three simple relaxation exercises' on pages 20–21) may be performed while lying down.

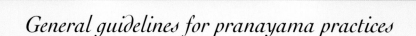

General guidelines for pranayama practices

These also apply to yoga practices

Sequence: Pranayama is usually performed after yoga *asanas* or physical relaxation exercises, and before meditation practice.

Posture: A comfortable sitting meditation posture.

Bathing: Wash the hands, face, and feet before starting.

Empty stomach: As with yoga *asana* practices, wait at least 3–4 hours after meals before starting pranayama. Food in the stomach puts pressure on the diaphragm and lungs, which impedes full, deep respiration.

Breathing style: Always breathe through the nose. Remain aware of the nostrils — when inhaling, the nostrils should dilate or 'flare;' when exhaling, they relax back to their natural position.

Pace: A relaxed, slow, steady pace is essential, so do not hurry through any aspects of the practice.

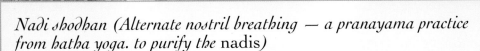

Nadi shodhan (Alternate nostril breathing — a pranayama practice from hatha yoga. to purify the nadis)

1. Sit in any comfortable meditation posture.

2. Keep the spine, neck and head upright and aligned.

3. Relax the whole body, and close the eyes.

4. Practice the Full Yogic Breath (abdomen to chest) for some minutes.

5. Rest both hands on the knees.

6. With the right hand:
   ◆ Place the fingers of the right hand in front of the face.
   ◆ Rest the index and middle fingers gently in between the eyebrows. Both fingers should be relaxed.
   ◆ With the thumb, close the right nostril, blocking the air flow.
   ◆ The ring finger rests adjacent to the left nostril.
   ◆ Breathing naturally, inhale and exhale five times through the left nostril. Be aware of each breath.
   ◆ After 5 breaths, release the thumb pressure on the right nostril, and press the left nostril with the ring finger.
   ◆ Breathing normally, inhale and exhale five times through the right nostril.
   ◆ Lower the hand to your knee, and breathe 5 times through both nostrils.

This constitutes one round. Practice five rounds, or for five minutes, ensuring that there is no sound as the air passes through the nostrils. Try to practice this for at least fifteen days. To build on its benefits, include it in your meditation practice at least a few times a week.

SOUND AND AROMA IN MEDITATION
Sound and the breath

Sound is the force which groups all things from atoms to worlds.
Hazrat Inayat Khan

Since the dawn of time, sound, like the breath from which it emanates, has come to denote life. From the breath comes the word, from the word comes the song, from the word and the song come the languages that reach out to communicate with the cosmos, and with life itself. It could be said that breath is the first mantra, word the first prayer, song the first music.

Life is unimaginable without music. Without the sounds that soothe and inspire us, life would become tedious beyond our ability to bear it. Perhaps the omniscient One understood this, and so music was created, as the wise ancients have said, to offer us relief from our sorrows and hardships.

Music has the power to transform. Since civilization began, the medium of sound has, in both its sacred and mundane forms, been used for purposes of healing, and for meditation. It has been used to induce feelings of reverence and transcendence in our most sacred religious rituals and festivals.

Today, we weave music into our private rituals, our entertainment, our celebrations, our birthing, our dying. Almost every aspect of our lives incorporates music in some way — 'wallpaper' music is even piped into elevators and shopping malls. Life today is unthinkable without the ubiquitous presence of music. Now, we usually have to go away from human presence — into the garden, the park, the wilderness, the desert — if we wish to experience silence!

In these days of easy accessibility to all types of sound and music through sophisticated reproduction technology, we can sometimes lose sight of the way that the ancients revered the nature of sound as a manifestly divine gift. Shamans (native healers), from the earliest hunter-gatherer cultures into the present, have used sound to travel into inner space on healing missions to contact spirits and guides.

One of the most remarkable discoveries of the ancient Indian sages was the insight, gleaned from their mystical experiences, that the universe is an ocean of vibration (*spanda*). The insights of these sages were documented in the ancient pre-Christian sacred texts known as the Vedas. The heart of the Vedic revelation is the sacred monosyllable OM. In a later Hindu sacred text, which followed the Vedas, came the declaration that the sonic Absolute can be heard as the sacred sound OM in deep meditation.

The sacred OM has now become known all over the planet as the quintessential mantra. Today, as in the past, the true believer who seeks transcendence and union with the Divine through sound faithfully chants the mantra OM within the quiet of his or her own heart and mind. Om, pronounced as Aum, recurs in the major religions: to Christians and Jews as Amen, to Muslims as Amin, and to Hindus and Buddhists as Om/Aum.

The mantra

A mantra is a word or phrase that is continuously repeated as an aid to meditation. It is a technique used in many traditions, such as Hinduism, Tibetan Buddhism, Sufism, Judaism and Christianity, among others. In this practice, the aim is to unite the mind with the sound of the chosen mantra. Individual, private repetition of a mantra and group chanting of a mantra are the two most prevalent uses of sound in meditation.

In contemporary cultures, the word mantra is increasingly being used to mean almost any repetitive word or phrase, which divorces the word from its inherent purpose. What is vitally missing in this mechanistic view of mantras is the understanding that the potential of the mantra is only released through meaningful intention and application by the one saying it. In simple terms, it is not what you say but the way that you say it.

Some of the best-known mantras, from different traditions, are:

In Hinduism: Names of God such as Shiva, Ram, Vishnu, and Krishna are common, such as in the mantra of the International Society of Krishna Consciousness: HARE RAMA HARE RAMA, RAMA RAMA HARE HARE, HARE KRISHNA HARE KRISHNA, KRISHNA KRISHNA HARE HARE.

OM NAMAH SHIVAYA ('OM, obeisance to Shiva').

RADHE GOVINDA ('O Radha and Govinda') — Govinda is a name of Krishna and Radha is his divine spouse. (This mantra unites male and female energetic aspects.)

TAT TVAM ASI ('You Are That').

All of these mantras aim to affirm one's essential identity with the Divine One. These mantras are also used in singing or chanting practices, which are called *Kirtan*. The essential aspect of *Kirtan* is that it is a devotional practice using mantras that contain the name/s of God.

In Tibetan Buddhism: The mantra 'Om Mani (or Mane) Padme Hum' ('OM, Hail to the jewel in the Lotus') is often used. This is pronounced by the Tibetans as OM MANI PEME HUNG.

In orthodox Christianity: The prayer: 'LORD JESUS CHRIST, SON OF GOD, HAVE MERCY ON ME, A SINNER' is used in a similar way to the mantra.

In Islam: LA ILAHA ILLA'LLAH ('There is no God but God'). In the Sufi mystical tradition of Islam, this is known as a *zikr* (or *dhikr*), which needs to be recited with 'the tongue of the heart.'

In Judaism: The intonations of Shalom ('Greetings') can be used in mantric form.

Meditation using the mantra 'Om'

The mantra OM is pronounced in three syllables: A - U - M.

◆ Sit comfortably in a meditation posture (*see* page 17).
◆ Close your eyes and breathe naturally.
◆ To settle and relax, focus on the breath for a few moments.
◆ Breathe into and release any tension areas in the body.
◆ Take a deep breath into your abdomen.
◆ Pronounce the first sound: a long A (as in A-A-A or Ah-Ah-Ah), and allow the sound to vibrate in your abdomen.
◆ Pronounce the second sound: a long U (as in O-O-O), moving your breath and attention to the chest area.
◆ Allow the sound to vibrate in the middle of the chest — the spiritual heart area.
◆ Pronounce the third sound: a long M (as in M-M-M), moving your focus to the nasal passages and to the area between your eyebrows (the third eye area), and allow the sound to vibrate in your 'third eye.'
◆ After the full exhalation of sound, again take a deep breath into your abdomen.
◆ Repeat the mantra process above.
◆ Feel the ascension of the sound and the vibrations throughout your body.
◆ Continue for ten minutes, if you can — or at least a dozen or so times.

If you enjoy the mantra practice and wish to continue it over a period of time, and when you feel confident with the sounds and the vibrational energy, try saying the mantra on the inhalation as well as the exhalation, so the recitation of the mantra becomes continuous.

Musical meditation for listening

Music is a wonderful meditation object because of the empathy most people feel towards their favorite compositions or musical genres.

Select a musical piece that you like. It can be any type of music, though preferably non-vocal, as the lyrics can take your mind into analytical mode.

Clear compositions, from any genre, are good because they give your mind instrumental variation on which to concentrate. This is a very pleasurable type of meditation, so enjoy it fully.

- Cue the music in the CD player, tape recorder, or DVD.
- Sit in your preferred, comfortable meditation posture.
- Take a few deep breaths and relax.
- Scan your body for any tense areas, breathe into them and release tension.
- Breathe deeply and naturally for a few moments.
- Turn on the music and give it your full concentration.
- Let yourself sink into the music — but remain alert.
- Notice the different sounds and instruments, notice how the sound weaves together.
- Notice the vibrations in your body, and where the different sounds resonate in your body.
- If images or other sensory material arises, notice it as part of the meditation, but try not to allow it to pull you off track.
- If your attention wanders, bring it back to the music.
- If you lose yourself in the music, rather than in a distraction, and are startled when you 'return,' or are surprised to find yourself suddenly at the end of your meditation, this is called absorption — a sign of progress!

A selection of music for meditation, relaxation and healing

Riley Lee (shakuhachi flute): *Yearning for The Bell* (projected series of 7 CDs — Vol 1–4 currently available), *Nalu — Moon Rider, As The Water Flows, Water Music, Wild Honey Dreaming*

Aeoliah (various instruments): *Inner Sanctum*

Deva Premal and Miten (voice, other): *The Essence, Love is Space* (contemporary renditions of traditional chants)

Ketil Bjornstad and David Darling (piano, cello): *The River*

Nawang Khechog (flute): *Rhythms of Peace*

Harold Budd and Brian Eno (spacious piano, synthesizer, other): *The Pearl* (with Daniel Lanois); *Ambient One: Music for Airports, Ambient Two: The Plateaux of Mirror, Apollo: Atmospheres & Soundtracks* (Brian Eno, Daniel Lanois, Roger Eno)

Paul Horn (flute, saxophone, other): *Inside The Great Pyramid, Inside the Taj Mahal, Nomad* (for listening meditation)

Deuter (Chaitanya Hari; flute, other): *Aum, Ecstasy, Silence is the Answer*

Henry Wolff and Nancy Hennings: *Tibetan Bells, Tibetan Bells II, Tibetan Bells III: The Empty Mirror*

Tony Scott: *Music for Zen Meditation; Meditation, Music for Yoga Meditation and Other Joys*

David Hykes and the Harmonic Choir: *Harmonic Meetings*

R. Carlos Nakai (flute): *Sundance Season*

Steve Roach: *Quiet Music, Structures from Silence*

Therese Schroeder-Sheker (harp, voice, cello and other): *Rosa Mystica* (for healing and transitions)

Genres: Gregorian Chant — for healing

Also check out the catalogs of these music companies:
Celestial Harmonies
Real World
New World Music

Meditation and aroma

All of our senses can be used in meditation as avenues to expand awareness. The olfactory sense, or sense of smell, is perhaps the most elusive to describe in any detail, yet we are daily absorbing subtle (and some not so subtle) aromas that stealthily influence our functioning and perceptions. To quote the ancient Greek philosopher Theophrastus: *'Every plant, animal or inanimate thing has an odor and one peculiar to itself, but in many cases it is not obvious to us. Thus things which appear to us to have no odor give forth one of which other animals are conscious.'*

Essential oils — extracted from the flowers, leaves, resins and barks of plants — have been used for thousands of years in religious rituals and for the purposes of healing, relaxation and meditation. Today, the practice of aromatherapy is one of the most popular of the complementary therapies. As well as its nurturing and pleasurable aspects, it helps people to revitalize their sense of smell.

Aromatherapy and meditation are inherently different practices; however, certain natural properties in incense and in essential oils, and their wondrous aromas, are used to purify an atmosphere, to generate a particular mood, and at the same time draw on their inherent subtle healing properties.

To experiment using essential oils and incense, try some of the suggestions in the following chart. After selecting one or two, use them as part of creating your meditation space and mood. You may also wish to try burning oils at other selected times to enhance a mood or to perfume a space, or to use the oils in bathing for their relaxing and therapeutic properties.

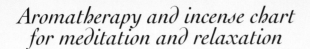

Aromatherapy and incense chart for meditation and relaxation

Frankincense (or *Olibanum*)	Said to deepen meditation. Traditionally used during rituals in religious places of worship.
Patchouli	Extremely popular oil in the East. Sensuous, pleasing fragrance.
Rose	Lovely fragrance with a peaceful aura. Has a balancing and calming effect upon the emotions, and is helpful in devotional practices. One of the most popular and useful essential oils.
Sandalwood	Since ancient times has traditionally been used for meditation. Has the power to inspire and elevate the consciousness. It is the basis of most incense preparations.
Jasmine	Is prepared from millions of tiny blossoms. A beautiful and very popular aroma. Said to uplift and assist receptive energies.
Lemongrass	Assists with concentration and psychic work.
Neroli (*Orange blossom*)	One of the finest flower essences. Uplifting, stabilizes the nervous system, calms and slows the mind.
Ylang-ylang	Beautiful, exotic fragrance, known as the 'flower of flowers.' Beneficial for the nervous system. Suitable for evening meditation.

Practice note: Constant use of one type of fragrance can arouse similar responses and feelings as those experienced on previous occasions. If you reserve particular essential oils, incense or types of fragrant candles for meditation and relaxation, it gradually becomes easier to relax and to move into the meditative alpha state more quickly, which enables you to advance to deeper levels in your meditation.

VISUALIZATION AND MEDITATION

The nature of visualization

Now I have my memory. But now you are blind. I am the guide into the sacred mountains. I will take you there. There is a great medicine lake there. The most beautiful lake in the world. All the world is reflected there. The people, the lodges of the people, and all the beings of the prairies and skies.

Hyemeyohts, Storm

Visualization is essentially the active use of the imagination to invoke certain qualities, elements or forces, and direct these towards certain goals. Some traditions, such as certain schools of Tibetan Buddhism, at times employ visualization as an adjunct to meditation to call upon spiritual forces that foster the process of spiritual attainment. However, the practices of meditation and visualization are really quite different, although they can complement one another.

In visualization, you are feeding your mind with specific information to follow, often with a defined aim, whereas in meditation, you are simply observing what happens, while maintaining a single focus of attention. The rise in popularity of visualization in the West is in large measure due to contemporary psychological research, which has demonstrated its effectiveness in self-development and in improving health. Visualization has been found to help us accomplish tasks, relate to the symptoms of discomfort and disease and to overcome personal barriers created by the beliefs we hold.

When we visualize, we draw on imagery from the conscious, the subconscious and the unconscious parts of our mind, and we do this in different ways:

◆ Through memory, by drawing on sensory impressions from the everyday world.

◆ Through each of our senses, which helps our inner world to come alive.

◆ Through the organising ability of our mind, which provides us with visual images that can have personal meaning.

◆ Through our emotions, which help us engage with the images we are seeing in 'the mind's eye.'

If you would like to experiment with visualization, you might try an exercise from this chapter, or from Meditating with Color (see pages 58–63). Choose one or two that particularly appeal to you, and/or that address certain needs. Experiment a few times so that you can become familiar enough with a visualization so it can flow. And, as with meditation, it is best to stick to one exercise for a while so your mind can settle, and it becomes possible for you to become absorbed in the practice.

Several practitioners of visualization have suggested that three important factors should be taken into account in order to direct the power of the imagination towards certain aims:

1. You must really believe that what you imagine will happen.

2. To facilitate manifestation, you need to visualize the desired object regularly.

3. You need to picture the means of obtaining the desired result as well as the goal itself.

Visualizing happiness and success

The renowned leader of the Tibetan people, Tenzin Gyatso, His Holiness the Fourteenth Dalai Lama, says often to audiences around the world: 'I believe that the very purpose of our life is to seek happiness.' The Dalai Lama spreads his message by being a *living* example of happiness. His usually smiling, friendly presence sparks warmth, humor and good will wherever he goes. In this way, he shows us all that happiness is possible to attain. The way to attain happiness, according to all the wisdom teachings, is to still the mind, to be kind to yourself and to others, to work towards resolving inner conflicts so that your outer actions express your inner being, and to know your true Self. This then leads not only to happiness but to real freedom. If you wish to find happiness, first of all you need to be very specific about what you mean by happiness. Your task is then to visualize, in your mind's eye, that you are already happy. This means visualizing your thoughts, your actions and your relationships with other people *now that you are happy*. You achieve success by becoming what you aspire to be in your mind's eye.

You train your mind and achieve inner peace through meditation. Then, at a certain stage, you let it all go — or rather, surrender in trust to the greater process at work. Along the journey, it is also great to have role models, but you should seek to manifest the inner qualities they personify, rather than the surface image; otherwise you may find that happiness and success are short-lived and ultimately unsatisfying. Above all, learn to trust your own experience, and go with what is true for you.

The chakras

A practice considered important by many schools of meditation and yoga is the awakening and purification of the *chakras*. The chakras are seven subtle energy centres in the body, and they are aligned with the spinal column. Chakras are associated with particular qualities, body areas, functions, and feelings. They work on several levels of our existence — the physical level, the mental or astral level, and the higher spiritual level. The *nadis*, the pathways through which *prana*, the life force, flows, weave in and around the chakras. Certain colors are also associated with the chakras, though these can vary in different belief systems.

Simple chakra meditation

Begin with the basic breath meditation. Then simply focus your attention on one chakra (or the particular area of a chakra), and let its qualities and characteristics reveal themselves to you. Meditate on one chakra at a time, and stay with each for a while so you can work with what arises. You may wish to begin at the base chakra, or muladhara, and work your way upwards, or you may be moved to focus on particular chakras at different times. Let your inner knowing guide your direction.

Another version of this is using the chakra chart, visualize each chakra in turn — from the first to the seventh — and flood each chakra with its designated color.

Chakra chart for meditation

Chakra	Location	Associated with	Properties/Represents
Muladhara (*or First/Root Chakra*)	Base of the spine. Is the seat of consciousness and operates on the physical sensation level.	Earth as 'Mother;' the color red or yellow (energy, vitality).	The unconscious, seat of the *kundalini.*[1]
Swadhistana (*or Second Chakra*)	Over the spleen, the genital region. The first developmental stage of the human.	Water, the color orange or silver (activity, energy, optimism, self-awareness).	Social; the subconscious; the development of knowledge.
Manipura (*or Third Chakra*)	On the inner side of the spinal column behind the navel.	Fire; the color yellow or red (energy, self-esteem, self-awareness).	Intellectual; inner security/safety.
Anahata (*or Fourth Chakra*)	At the level of the physical heart, in the center of the chest.	Air; the color green or blue (grounding, centering, harmonising).	Acquisitive; understanding, love, devotion, compassion, forgiveness.
Vishuddi (*or Fifth Chakra*)	In the throat.	Ether or space; the color blue or indigo (clarity, the voice, creative expression).	Purification — physical (nutrients, radiation, poisons/toxins) and psychical (the control of words and feelings, patience); seat of sound.
Ajna (*or Sixth Chakra*)	Commonly said to be between the eyebrows but is around the top of the spinal column.	The spiritual; the color violet or white (as the complement to black) — purity, clarity, spirituality.	Intuition; boundary between human and divine consciousness; the 'third eye'; unity.
Sahasrara (*or Seventh Chakra*)	The crown of the head.	In the West, the color violet — spirituality; in the East, is colorless.	Free of properties. Represents pure consciousness (union of the individual soul with the Divine/God) Self-Realization, bliss, imperturbable inner peace, liberation.

MEDITATING WITH COLOR

Color as phenomena with varying levels or 'wave-like' frequencies of vibration

Color is not in an object itself — it is due to the light shining onto it …
a beam of light is really a [wave-like] stream of tiny glowing particles.
Sir Isaac Newton

In 1672, the scientist Sir Isaac Newton displayed memorably to the West that when pure white light passes through a prism it breaks up into seven colors — what is now commonly called the rainbow color spectrum. All phenomena are varying levels or 'wave-like' frequencies of vibration. In these terms, the rainbow colors range from red at the 'long wave-length' or 'low-frequency' end of the scale, through to violet at the 'short wave-length' or 'high-frequency' end. Collectively, these spectral or prismatic colors — red, orange, yellow, green, blue, indigo, and violet — represent varying vibrational qualities of pure white light. They have many different applications in meditation and healing.

Some meditation practices link particular colors of the rainbow spectrum to each of the seven *chakras*, or subtle energy centers, in the body (*see* 'Chakra chart for meditation' on page 57). Variations exist in these color ascriptions; for example, in the West, the color violet is associated with the chakra situated at the crown of the head, the *sahasrara*. In the East, the color violet is associated with the 'third eye,' or *ajna* chakra, situated between the eyebrows. Eastern countries also perceive gold and orange to have spiritual significance, which is why monks' and swamis' robes are colored gold/orange.

The natural phenomenon of a rainbow is a rapturous sight. The rainbow spectrum itself has come to symbolize a harmonising of different elements. A mandala is a symbol often used in meditation and in healing. The mandala has many levels of meaning, but overall it has come to signify integration and wholeness. To meditate with awareness upon the rainbow spectrum as a mandala in the body can be a wonderfully nourishing experience.

Color perception is very subjective, and is as much an internal visual experience as an external one. However, red, orange and yellow are often seen as vitalizing and heat-producing colors, while blue, indigo and violet are seen as cooler, more calming colors. Green, which is positioned in the center of the color spectrum, and is sometimes associated with the heart chakra, or *anahata*, is often considered the color of harmony and balance.

We can use different colors for healing by, for example, visualizing a specific colored light — such as gold, green, or violet — entering our body with the breath. We all carry around negative thoughts and depleting emotions — which we can visualize as black — that can be released as 'black smoke' on an exhalation. Color breathing visualizations can provide a creative approach to dissipating negativity as well as renewing a positive attitude and overall sense of well-being.

With color-breathing techniques, you can select different colors for different problems.

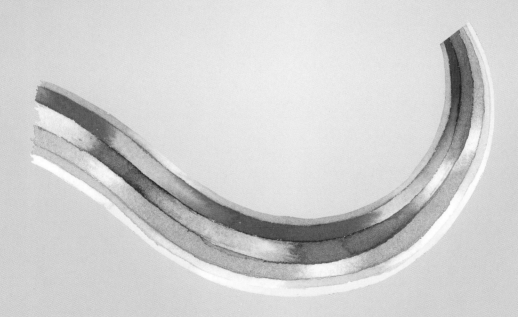

Color breathing for healing

Choose either white light or a color that symbolizes healing. In your selection, take into account what it is you want to heal. Is it a physical, emotional or mental concern? Check out what different colors generally represent, and check in with yourself to see what color/s feel right for the problem.

- Sit in a comfortable position with your spine, neck and head aligned.
- Take a few minutes to relax completely (see 'Three simple relaxation exercises' on pages 20–21).
- Breathe naturally, deeply and rhythmically.
- Close your eyes and visualize the color you have selected, and allow it to grow in your mind's eye (or ajna chakra — between your eyebrows).
- If the color seems unclear at first, or begins to blend with another color, persist until the color is pure and true in your inner vision. If, after a few minutes, a clear color doesn't emerge, visualize white light.
- Now imagine your entire body being bathed in the healing balm of that particular color, or in radiant white light.
- Maintain a pattern of breathing deeply and rhythmically, and imagine the color being drawn into your solar plexus (or manipura chakra) with each inward breath.
- Now visualize the healing color spreading throughout your body. If there is a part of your body that particularly requires healing, visualize the color entering this area, transmitting its healing properties to that part. If more than one part needs healing, direct the healing color to each part in turn.
- Then, with each outward breath, visualize the toxins or dis-ease elements leaving your body.
- Continue the breathing for at least ten minutes, or until you feel a sense of being cleansed or purified.
- Complete your visualization with an expression of gratitude, or an affirmation of your positive health and well-being.

Practice note: These exercises need to be practiced regularly for enduring benefits. To visualize regaining health after illness, try picturing the body bathed in green, blue, gold or violet light. There are a range of color-healing exercises available, but if you are ever in any doubt about which color to choose, use white light — as it is the primal source of all color, white is the most universally applied 'color' in visualizations for transformative purposes.

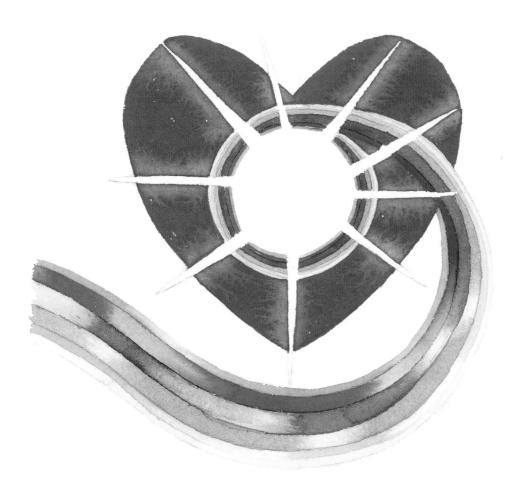

A rainbow mandala meditation

We can use the rainbow spectrum in a different way, by visualizing it as a 'color wheel' of six prismatic colors — red, orange, yellow, green, blue, and violet. When we do this, we imagine that the complementary colors are opposite each other — red opposite green, blue opposite orange, yellow opposite violet. In this way, the colors don't cancel each other out. We will use this color wheel as a 'rainbow mandala' for our meditation.

The exercise is in two stages: the first stage is a simple color visualization of the body, to acclimatize the imagination; the second stage is the rainbow mandala visualization. The stages can also be done individually, though it is important to become familiar with Stage One before progressing.

Stage One:

- Begin by lying down and closing your eyes.
- Take a few deep breaths and relax.
- Visualize different sections, organs and functions of your body in terms of particular colors — for example, picture your head, throat, chest, lungs, breathing, heart, blood circulation, the abdomen, sexual organs, and feet. See which colors appear as you do this. Don't force it — just see which colors come naturally.
- When you have become used to visualizing various parts of your body as different colors, try Stage Two of this visualization, which is picturing your body as a rainbow mandala.

Stage Two:

- Focus on your heart as a center of vibrant white light, and then imagine the six complementary colors of your rainbow mandala moving slowly out in all directions and filling your entire body.
- Imagine your arms and legs as defining the perimeter of the mandala.
- Now visualize the color as energy, vitalizing each and every cell, and the color energy

filling your entire body, then extending outwards in a wonderful circle of colored light — a rainbow circle of peace and harmony. Now focus on this rainbow circle so the warmest part of the color spectrum is radiating from your heart, and the coolest part extends towards the edge of your body. Now imagine that the rainbow mandala is reaching out still further — extending to the area surrounding your body. Focus your thoughts on the pulsing light radiating through your rainbow mandala. Notice any particular thoughts, emotions or memories that may arise at this time.

◆ Now imagine that the colors of your rainbow mandala are slowly returning to their source in your heart center. Imagine that the different colors are once again combining to produce pure white light. Now imagine that this pure white light is filling your body — filling it so completely that you are no longer sure of your body outline. Focus on simply being pure, white light — the source of all color, the source of all — which is now dissolving all impurities. Bathe in this light and feel its revitalizing power bringing you a deep sense of inner peace.

(Adapted from Jose and Mirium Arguelles, *Mandala* (1972).)

To close this meditation, you may choose to imagine this pure white light, or a rainbow spectrum, surrounding your body like a protective shell or sphere. You feel completely safe here, and you are being nourished and nurtured by the healing qualities of the pure, white light.

The therapeutic use of color

Healing with color has long been a universal art. The ancient Egyptians associated different-colored light with each of their gods and goddesses, and also with different seasons and specific times of the day. Color healing is practiced by the Chinese, the Indians, and the indigenous peoples of North and South America. Today, color therapy is a popular Western modality in natural health care.

Meditation and Movement
Movement meditations

And everything comes to one, as we dance on, dance on, dance on.
Theodore Roethke

Movement meditations — such as walking, dancing, Sufi whirling and Tai Chi — are just as effective at clearing the mind and focusing your attention, if you perform these activities with mindfulness; that is, being conscious of everything that arises from within and without. Movement meditations are particularly suited to those who find it difficult, or counterproductive, to sit still. They are also helpful practices for all meditators, as they help you take your meditation practice into everyday life, which is an important goal of all true meditation.

Some movement meditations, such as Tai Chi or Falun Gong, require tuition from an experienced teacher; however, a few practices are simple and, while they require patience to develop, can be performed by anyone. One of these practices is a Zen walking meditation known as Kinhin.

If you choose to practice Kinhin, try to remember, as with your other meditation practices, not to become discouraged if it takes you a little time to get the hang of it. Perhaps surprisingly, even proficiency in martial arts demands the relaxed, alert awareness of the meditative mind. The essence of effective martial arts, as with any meditative activity, is in finding the balance and harmony between inner awareness and outer movement.

Walking meditation (Kinhin)

Choose an area that allows you to walk straight ahead for at least a dozen short paces. This could be in your home, in the garden, in the park — anywhere you will not be disturbed.

◆ Make a fist with your left hand. Keep it turned so that your thumb faces inward.
◆ Placing your right hand over your left and exert gentle pressure against your abdomen, just below the navel.
◆ Look at the ground ahead.
◆ Now lift either your right or left foot, with total attention on each movement in the ankle and leg, and the sensation in the sole of the foot.
◆ Take a very short pace forward and put your foot on the ground, feeling the new sensations under the sole.
◆ Take further paces, with the same awareness. Go as far as you can, then retrace your steps.
◆ Keep your movements slow and deliberate, yet smooth and flowing throughout.
◆ The focus of attention is on your legs and feet.

The same basic principles apply in movement meditations as in meditation generally, i.e.:
Relaxation of the body.
Single-pointed focus of attention.
Natural breathing (except when otherwise instructed).
Bringing the mind gently back to the meditation object when attention strays.
Noting intrusions, but allowing everything to pass through.
Letting go of everything other than your meditation — including, and most of all, your ego-bound self.

Dance and meditation: dancing meditation

To dance is to celebrate life. To *really* dance, with full attention on the dance itself, is to connect with something primal within you. Dance is a wonderful way to let go, to release, and to immerse yourself totally in an activity. Something joyous, cathartic and liberating is created by the act of dancing that is difficult to experience in other forms of activity.

The difference between meditative dancing and other forms of dancing is the losing of oneself in the dance, rather than focusing on a technique. When that happens, meditation happens. However, to begin with, one needs a point of focus.

- Select some music that you love and that moves you to dance.
- Find a space that allows you freedom of movement without the possibility of hurting yourself by hitting an obstacle.
- Wear loose clothing that allows your body to breathe — natural fibers are best — and that does not restrict your movement in any way.
- Turn the music on, tune into the music, and let yourself dance in any way that your body wants to move.
- As a point of focus, you can: tune into the music and let the music itself move you; imagine that you are a child again, and are dancing for the sheer pleasure of it; imagine that you are dancing to God; imagine that you are dancing to a beloved — though without becoming self-conscious; dance as your spirit is moved to dance.
- Maintain your focus for the duration of the dance.
- At the close of your dance meditation, allow yourself a few minutes to be still and quiet by lying down or sitting quietly.
- Notice your energy and whatever else arises.
- Give thanks for the dance, and the music, and for this self-nourishing time.

A selection of music for dance meditation

Omar Faruk Tekbilik and Brian Keane: *Fire Dance*
Brian Keane: *Beyond the Sky*
Deuter (Chaitanya Hari): *Nirvana Road*
Deuter (Chaitanya Hari): *Celebration*
Babatunde Olatunji (and various artists): *Drums of Passion: The Beat*
Little Wolf Band: *Dream Song*
Peter Gabriel: *Passion: Music for The Last Temptation of Christ*
Peter Buffett: *500 Nations: A Musical Journey*
Kishna Das: *Pilgrim Heart*
Mihis Theodorakis: *Zorba The Greek*
Nusrat Fateh Ali Khan: *Devotional and Love Songs*
Nusrat Fateh Ali Khan: *The Last Prophet*
Nusrat Fateh Ali Khan: *Mustt Mustt*

Walking in nature meditations

We are the sap of stars, the fiber of earth, the soul of creation.
Anna Voigt

A profoundly healing form of movement meditation is simply walking in 'Mother Nature.' To be in Nature is a form of soul nourishment that is deeply rejuvenating, and, like dancing, renews our connection to the deeper and greater reality that moves life itself.

An increasingly popular Western form of movement meditation in Nature is walking 'the labyrinth' — or finding your way through 'the maze.' The structure of the labyrinth is symbolic of the journey of life, and arriving at the 'empty' center, which is the task and the goal of the walk, represents the arrival at the center of the self. If you have access to a labyrinth, try this journey for an interesting variation of your practice. However, if this is not an option for you, a beautiful and ancient movement meditation practice accessible to all is the simple experience of 'walking in the breeze.'

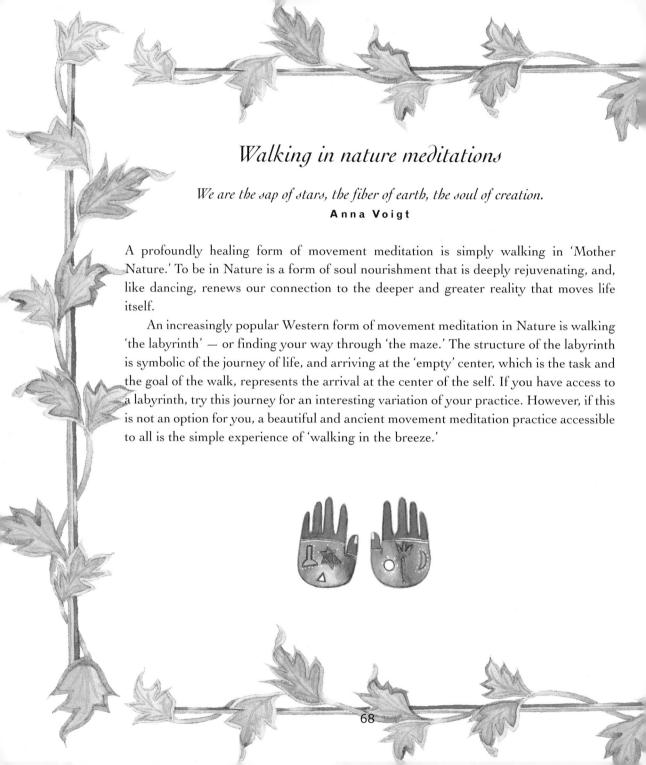

Walking in the breeze meditation

For this practice, choose a natural place in the open air, preferably somewhere quiet —
your garden, a park, the seaside — where you can walk for at least ten minutes, perhaps
barefoot, without being disturbed.

◆ Begin walking normally. Breathe deeply, rhythmically, and naturally.

◆ As you walk, feel the breeze on your skin, feel it in your hair, feel it in your being.
  Feel the touch of the breeze as it comes and goes. If the day is windy, notice the
  quality of the wind and its effect on your body; if the day is still, notice the subtle
  movement of air around you as you walk.

◆ Continue your walk with your attention on the breeze and how it feels on, and in,
  your body. If you become distracted, simply bring your attention back to the breeze.
  What can happen is that the breeze, your body, and your breathing become like one
  beautiful breath — but don't force it. Allow experiences to naturally and freely
  emerge of their own accord.

◆ Simply enjoy the beauty of it all.

TRADITIONAL MEDITATIONS

Three things cannot be long hidden, the sun, the moon, and the truth.

B u d d h a

You can certainly practice meditation without knowing its spiritual and historical roots, but it can be rewarding to contextualize some of the background to the meditative traditions. It can also be enriching to know that the simple practice of meditation has been a venerated sacred ritual for thousands upon thousands of years. Indeed, meditation practices, together with contemplation and prayer, exist in all of the world's great religions from East and West.

Shamanism

Shamanism, which has survived (albeit fractured and with fewer adepts) agriculture, industrialization, and the technological revolution, perceives the entire cosmos as being alive with all living forms as interconnected. It has been called the world's first great religion. Shamans, who were responsible for maintaining the health and harmony of their tribes, would (and still do) travel into inner space to seek spiritual assistance for ailing individuals, and for guidance on resolving tribal discordancies. Ancient cave and rock paintings in Europe and Australia attest to the trance voyages of the shamans.

Buddhism

Of all the world's great wisdom traditions, Buddhism is the most closely identified with meditation. Buddhism, on one level, sprouted from Hinduism. On another level, it grew from the great 'enlightenment' experience, about 2,500 years ago, of the thirty-five-year old Siddhartha Gautama, who became 'the Buddha' (the 'Awakened One'). Essentially, Siddhartha, after many years of practicing yoga and spiritual austerities, sat under a bo tree, at Bodh Gaya in eastern India, to turn inward and examine his own mind (i.e., to meditate). After forty-nine days (twenty-four hours, or seven days and nights — accounts vary), and after a series of inner encounters, he spontaneously attained 'enlightenment' — Nirvana or Moksha.

The Buddha taught his followers that meditation is essential to the unfolding of spiritual reality, and for each person to trust his or her own inner experiencing above all else. From India, Buddhism, through enlightened teachers, traveled to other parts of the East.

Buddhism has spawned many sects, some of which have found increasing popularity in the West — such as Zen Buddhism (which also contains aspects of the Chinese Tao), Vipassana ('insight' meditation), and, increasingly, various practices from Tibetan Buddhism.

Hinduism

Ancient India was the birthplace of meditation as we know it. In the remote Himalayas, the earliest known sacred scriptures on earth, the Hindu Vedas, which extend back about 5,000 years, were first documented. From Vedic and post-Vedic spirituality came the three most widely practiced meditative traditions in India — Yoga, Tantra and Buddhism. India itself can lay claim to having had more enlightened human beings, or saints, emerge from its land than anywhere else on earth.

One of the greatest souls of the twentieth century, Sri Ramana Maharshi, who passed on in 1950, taught that one could, if mature enough, 'awaken' simply by continuously asking the one perennial question, 'Who am I?.'

The Sufism of Islam

Sufism is widely regarded as the mystical expression of Islam, though some say its roots go back much further. It is a path of love and devotion to the Divine within, and its practioners seek, through specific practices, intimate and ecstatic union with the Beloved (God) within their own hearts. It is frequently called 'the Path of the Heart.'

One of Sufism's unique meditation practices is the whirling dance of the Mevlani order — the 'whirling dervishes.' Another Sufi meditation ritual is the *zikr* (or *dhikr*) — 'remembrance of God' — which is a constant repetition, or chant, of the name of God, or a sacred phrase, such as *La ila'ha, il'alahu* or *La ilaha illa'llah* ('there is no God but God'), while breathing deeply and rhythmically.

Judaism

The mystical element of Judaism is called the Kabbalah, and is said to date back to Abraham, the founder of Judaism. The Old Testament prophets are believed to have entered into meditative states through fasting and ascetic practices. However, the first formal Jewish meditation practice is said to be a concentrated focus on the Hebrew alphabet, perceived in Judaism as the divine language of God.

Jewish mediators, like other practitioners in other religions, use sacred scriptural phrases as mantras to focus the mind and to attain closeness to God. Perhaps the best-known Kabbalah meditation practice is concentration on the concepts of each of the ascending levels of the pictograph, the 'Tree of Life.' This symbolic map depicts the various levels through which God, 'the First Cause,' descends into, and creates, the material world. The 'Tree of Life' shows the 'innately flawed' and 'mechanical' human being how, by reversing God's descent, s/he can ascend the various levels of consciousness to attain inner equilibrium and communion with God.

Christianity

Mystical elements have existed in Christianity since the time of Jesus Christ. Jesus himself is said to have been been practicing a form of meditation when he fasted and prayed for forty days and nights in the desert. This event gave rise to the Christian practice known as contemplative prayer.

After the time of Jesus, the first Christian meditators are said to be the desert fathers who lived in Palestine and Egypt in the 3rd and 4th centuries. They lived mostly in physical isolation, seeking God's presence through the constant repetition of a sacred phrase. This practice was, in essence, carried on by the nuns, monks and other Christian mystics of medieval Europe.

The contemplative tradition, which is a variant of meditation, has remained strong in the Christian Orthodox Churches of Russia, Greece and Eastern Europe. The technique that was most frequently used by churches was a type of mantra recitation, the repetition of the prayer: 'Lord Jesus Christ, Son of God, have mercy on me, a sinner.' The phrases from the Gospel of John can also be used as mantras: 'I am the light of the world' and 'I am the way, the truth, and the life.'

Many similarities exist in all of the mystical traditions from East and West, most notably that the divine is in each human being, and can be experienced through the sustained practice of turning within, in devoted one-focused meditation and contemplation.

Where the far Eastern and Western religions differ is that in the latter, God is seen as a separate entity who exists outside of the 'flawed' human being and outside of Nature. A believer can come to know God, but not unite with God. Inherently dualistic, Western tradition relies on *dogma* to reinforce belief. By contrast, the Eastern perspective, along with the Western mystical traditions, advocates that through *experience*, any human being, as a spark of the Divine, can attain God-Realization through complete surrender of the small ego-self to absorption in the Divine within, so that what remains is only the One/God.

However, any sincere and devoted seeker can realize the true Self, or come to know the God within — irrespective of the path (though it helps to have guidance and spiritual friends on the way). Also, in most mystical traditions, all practices — at a certain point — fall away as one loses all sense of the individual self in the divine bliss of union. In this way, all paths lead to the One.

As essentially a non-denominational practice, meditation can be practiced by anyone. Many people, coming from various religions, have commented that meditation has served both to deepen their awareness and to enrich their existing religious practices. So, in essence, meditation exists as a directly spiritual practice as well as a secular means of attaining greater health, equilibrium, and inner peace.

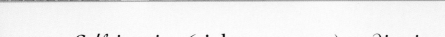

Self-inquiry (vichara marga) meditation

The Self-inquiry meditation is based on the traditional Hindu practice of *vichara marga*, the path of inquiry, or 'Self-inquiry.' Essentially, this is a practice of simply, and repeatedly, asking within yourself the question 'Who am I?' and holding this thought alone, with a completely open and receptive mind as to any answers, responses or sensations that may arise.

1. Sit comfortably, take a few deep breaths, and slowly exhale, releasing any tension with the out-breath.
2. Close your eyes and turn your attention inward.
3. Inwardly and quietly, and with an open mind and heart, ask yourself: Who am I? — without demanding a response. Patiently attend to your breathing while noticing what arises.
4. When other thoughts arise, do not pursue them but simply inquire of each thought — 'To whom has this thought arisen?' If the answer comes — 'To me,' then you repeat the question: Who am I?
5. Attend to your breathing throughout the meditation and, from time to time, repeat the question, in a relaxed way, without any expectations of an anwer.

This is an excellent meditation that can be easily incorporated into your basic breathing meditations. It is particularly useful for those who are inclined to rely too much on, or who are preoccupied with, thinking.

INCORPORATING MEDITATION TECHNIQUES INTO A BUSY WORKING DAY

Bringing equilibrium, detachment and calm

*Blessed are the footsteps of those who bring
the message of peace over the mountains.*

from a rendition of the Manu Vu in *The Book of Isaiah*

This quote may seem at odds with the title of this chapter; however, its message is about developing an inner calm that can extend to smoothing the sometimes choppy waters of exterior life, wherever you may be. This is an attitude of mind that can help carry you through the day with equanimity, dignity and lightness of being.

Contemporary living is characterized by its unprecedented speed of change, its complexity, and its chaotic 'busyness' — often to the point of eroding our health, well-being, and joy. As one commentator put it, we are constantly distracted by distraction. Meditation works counter to this in simplifying life, in providing a space to shift from thinking to sensing, and in helping us to attend to our inner experiences. It enables us to hear our intuition, and to discover the beauty that resides in 'stillness' and 'silence.'

To bring some detachment and ease into our pressured working lives, we need to apply the skills and information that we learn in our private relaxation and meditation practices to all aspects of our lives. In other words, we need to make each passing moment of the journey of life a meditation experience. Such a practice is also the path to freedom.

When an elephant is free, it moves its trunk
and looks restless, but if it is given a chain to hold,
its trunk stays still.
Similarly, without an aim, the mind is restless.
If an aim is fixed, it is restful... When we can get the mind
to stick to one thought, the energy is conserved and the mind becomes stronger.
Strength of mind is gained by practice.

Sri Ramana Maharshi

Useful tips to help you in a pressured working life

Tip One: Meditate each and every day

Even if only for a few minutes. If you are unable to meditate first thing in the morning, then before leaving your bed, quietly and sincerely resolve to yourself that you will move through the day with calm, balance, response-ability, simplicity, detachment, and a light touch. If you can conjure an image that to you symbolizes these qualities, use that as an anchor or reference point (e.g., a tree can be a 'grounding' symbol). Then move serenely into your day.

Tip Two: Take brief 'rest-breaks'

Try taking short 'refresher' breaks during the day, whenever you have a moment or two. In other words, utilize the space in between things to take a respite. This is not unlike the restful 'empty' space in between breathing in and breathing out. To take a short (but avoid calling it a 'quick') break:

◆ Close your eyes or let them rest softly on a visual object, simply listen to all the sounds around you, or focus on a sensation in your body.

◆ Take a deep breath into your belly, pause, and release a sigh (vocally or internally) — allowing your body to relax on the out-flowing breath.

◆ Maintain your focus for as long as your break allows, emptying your mind of all work and/or other thoughts — or letting them go if they arise.

◆ Return to your work. Repeat the process whenever you have an opportunity.

Tip Three: Work with your biorhythm cycle

When scheduling tasks and brief breaks, try to accommodate your natural energy 'highs' and 'lows.' For example, many people feel an energy lull around 4.00 P.M. This is a good time to take a short rest break when possible.

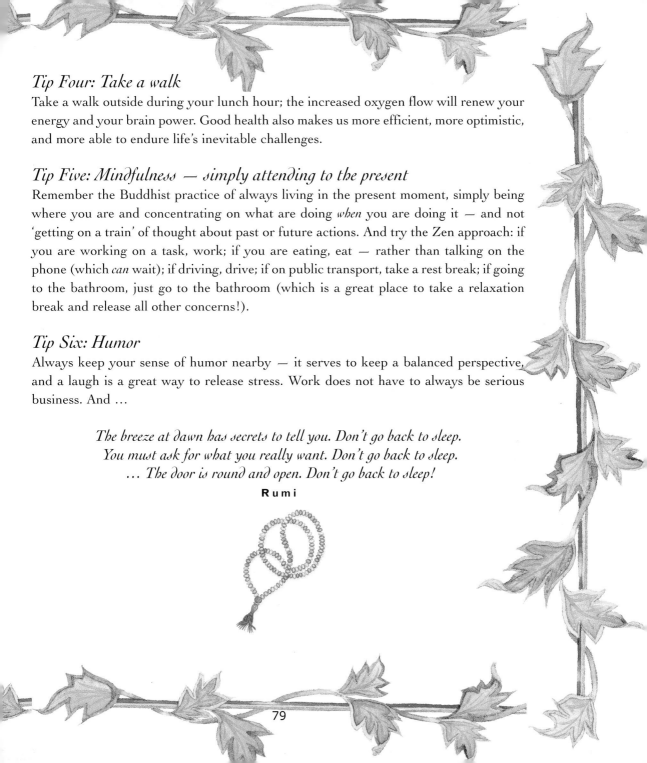

Tip Four: Take a walk

Take a walk outside during your lunch hour; the increased oxygen flow will renew your energy and your brain power. Good health also makes us more efficient, more optimistic, and more able to endure life's inevitable challenges.

Tip Five: Mindfulness — simply attending to the present

Remember the Buddhist practice of always living in the present moment, simply being where you are and concentrating on what are doing *when* you are doing it — and not 'getting on a train' of thought about past or future actions. And try the Zen approach: if you are working on a task, work; if you are eating, eat — rather than talking on the phone (which *can* wait); if driving, drive; if on public transport, take a rest break; if going to the bathroom, just go to the bathroom (which is a great place to take a relaxation break and release all other concerns!).

Tip Six: Humor

Always keep your sense of humor nearby — it serves to keep a balanced perspective, and a laugh is a great way to release stress. Work does not have to always be serious business. And …

The breeze at dawn has secrets to tell you. Don't go back to sleep.
You must ask for what you really want. Don't go back to sleep.
… The door is round and open. Don't go back to sleep!
Rumi

This edition published by Barnes & Noble, Inc.,
by arrangement with Lansdowne Publishing

2001 Barnes & Noble Books

M 10 9 8 7 6 5 4 3 2 1

ISBN 0-7607-2413-X

Published by Lansdowne Publishing Pty Ltd
Sydney NSW 2000, Australia

Commissioned by Deborah Nixon
Text: Anna Voigt
Illustrator: Sue Ninham
Designer: Robyn Latimer
Editor: Patricia Dacey
Production Manager: Sally Stokes
Project Co-ordinator: Alexandra Nahlous

Set in Cochin on QuarkXPress
Printed in Singapore by Tien Wah Press (Pte) Ltd